THEMATIC UNIT

Food and Nutrition

Written by Mary Ellen Sterling

Teacher Created Materials, Inc.
6421 Industry Way
Westminster, CA 92683
www.teachercreated.com

©2000 Teacher Created Materials, Inc.

Made in U.S.A.

ISBN-1-57690-373-7

Illustrated by
Ana Castanares

Edited by
Janet A. Hale, M.S. Ed.

Cover Art by
Cheri Macoubrie Wilson

Table of Contents

Introduction

Food and Nutrition contains a captivating whole language thematic unit. Its 80 exciting pages are filled with a wide variety of lesson ideas and activities designed for use with children at the primary level. For each of the three featured books—*Making Vegetable Soup*, *Bread Bread Bread*, and *Gregory the Terrible Eater*—activities are included which set the stage for reading, encourage the enjoyment of the book, and extend the concepts gained. In addition, the theme is connected to the curriculum with activities in language arts (including language experience and writing suggestions), math, science, art, music, and life skills (cooking, physical education, etc.). Many of these activities encourage cooperative learning. Suggestions and patterns for bulletin boards are additional timesavers for the busy teacher. Furthermore, directions for student-created big books and culminating activities highlight this very complete teacher resource.

This thematic unit includes:

- ❏ **literature selections**—summaries of three children's books with related lessons (complete with reproducible pages) that cross the curriculum

- ❏ **language experience and writing ideas**—suggestions as well as activities across the curriculum

- ❏ **bulletin board ideas**—suggestions and plans for student-created and/or interactive bulletin boards

- ❏ **homework suggestions**—extending the unit to the child's home

- ❏ **curriculum connections**—in language arts, math, science, art, music, and life skills such as cooking and physical education

- ❏ **group projects**—to foster cooperative learning

- ❏ **culminating activities**—which require students to synthesize their learning to produce a product or engage in an activity that can be shared with others

- ❏ **a bibliography**—suggesting additional literature and nonfiction books on the theme

---

> To keep this valuable resource intact so that it can be used year after year, you may wish to punch holes in the pages and store them in a three-ring binder.

Introduction (cont.)

Why a Balanced Approach?

The strength of a balanced language approach is that it encourages students to use all modes of communication—reading, writing, listening, and illustrating. Communication skills are interconnected and integrated into lessons that emphasize the whole of language. Implicit to this approach is the knowledge that every whole—including individual words—is composed of parts, and directed study of those parts can help a student master the whole. Experience and research tell us that regular attention to phonics, other word-attack skills, spelling, etc., helps develop reading mastery. Students should be regularly encouraged to read, write, spell, speak, and listen in response to a literature experience. In these ways, language skills grow rapidly, stimulated by direct practice, involvement, and interest in the topic at hand.

Why Thematic Planning?

One very useful tool for implementing an integrated whole language program is thematic planning. By choosing a theme with correlating literature selections for a unit of study, a teacher can plan activities throughout the day that lead to a cohesive, in-depth study of the topic. Students will be practicing and applying their skills in meaningful contexts. Consequently, they will tend to learn and retain more. Both teachers and students will be freed from a day that is broken into unrelated segments of isolated drill and practice.

Why Cooperative Learning?

Besides academic skills and content, students need to learn social skills. No longer can this area of development be taken for granted. Students must learn to work cooperatively in groups in order to function well in modern society. Group activities should be a regular part of school life, and teachers should consciously include social objectives as well as academic objectives in their planning. For example, a group working together to solve a problem may need to select a leader. The teacher should make clear to the students and monitor the qualities of good leader/follower group interaction just as he/she would state and monitor the academic goals of the project.

Why Big Books?

An excellent cooperative, whole language activity is the production of big books. Groups of students, or the whole class, can apply their language skills, content knowledge, and creativity to produce a big book that can become a part of the classroom library to be read and reread. These books make excellent culminating projects for sharing beyond the classroom with parents, librarians, and other classes, etc. big books can be produced in many ways, and this thematic unit book includes directions for at least one method you may choose.

Growing Vegetable Soup
by Lois Ehlert

Summary

It is time to grow vegetable soup. The tools are ready and the seeds and sprouts are planted. Water and sunlight help the plants grow. After weeding and watching the plants, it is time to pick them or dig them up. The plants are taken home where they are washed, cut up, and placed in a pot of water. Soon it is time to taste the vegetable soup. It is the best ever!

The outline below is a suggested plan for using the various activities that are presented in this unit. You should adapt these ideas to fit your own classroom situation.

Sample Plan

Lesson 1

- Prepare the Food Pyramid Bulletin Board (pages 68-75).
- Discuss the vegetables on display (page 6, Setting the Stage #3).
- Read *Growing Vegetable Soup*.

Lesson 2

- Review the story with sentence strips (page 8).
- Place the story vegetables in alphabetical order (page 9).
- Make a vegetable graph (page 11).

Lesson 3

- Sample fresh vegetables (page 6, Enjoying the Book #3).
- Use descriptions to tell about vegetables (page 9).
- Learn how we taste bitter, sour, salty, and sweet (page 52).

Lesson 4

- Make Vegetable Sculptures (page 10).
- Create some Fancy Treats with fresh vegetables (page 12).
- Send a note home for families to send vegetables for making soup (page 13).

Lesson 5

- Make vegetable soup (page 12).
- Write a class recipe for making soup (page 9).
- Learn about the difference between fruits and vegetables. Complete the coloring activity on page 14.

Overview of Activities

Setting the Stage

1. Prepare a special space or table area in your classroom for your *Food and Nutrition* unit. Find food-related books and materials (see the Bibliography on pages 79 and 80, as well as other resources found on page 78). A library media specialist may serve as a good resource for locating additional materials.

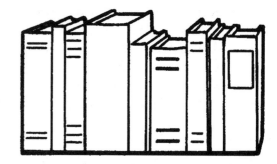

2. Set the mood in the classroom with a Food Pyramid Bulletin Board. See pages 68 to 75 for complete patterns and directions.

3. Display and label a variety of fresh vegetables on a special table. After a day or two, remove the labels and let the children match the labels with the correct vegetables.

4. Take the children on a field trip to a grocery store or farmer's market where they can see fresh vegetables up close. Make arrangements for the produce manager to show the vegetables to the class and to share some interesting facts about each one.

5. Plant a class vegetable garden. Some ideas for planting and tending a garden are provided on pages 48 and 49.

Enjoying the Book

1. Introduce the book *Growing Vegetable Soup* by calling attention to the display of vegetables. Ask the children to name each vegetable and then name the food group to which it belongs.

2. Cut apart the sentence strips on page 8 to review the story events. Make enough sets so that each pair of children or a small group of children can put the strips in correct story order.

3. Experience a variety of fresh vegetables. Discuss the vegetables named in the story *Growing Vegetable Soup*. Let the children examine the vegetables and use all their senses to describe them (including tasting the vegetables). Afterwards, have the children draw a picture of one of the vegetables and write a descriptive sentence about it.

My celery is green and bumpy and tastes crunchy.

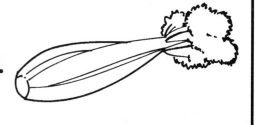

Overview of Activities *(cont.)*

Enjoying the Book *(cont.)*

4. Make vegetable sculptures (see page 10 for complete directions). Attach smaller vegetables to zucchini, potatoes, squash, eggplant, and carrots to make funny and amazing creatures. Ask the children to name their sculptures and identify the vegetables they used. Share the pictures from the book *Play with Your Food* by Joost Bliffers. The children will certainly enjoy the whimsical creatures depicted.

5. Cook some vegetables or eat them raw. Let the children taste a variety of vegetables from fresh to frozen vegetables and canned vegetables.

6. Construct a class graph of vegetable favorites. See page 11 for more information and how-tos on this project. To make a permanent, reusable graph see the directions on page 17 (Extending the Book, #3).

Vegetable	Votes					
tomato						
green bean						
carrot						

Extending the Book

1. Learn the differences between fruits and vegetables. Find out which vegetables are often referred to as fruits although they are actually vegetables. A coloring and visual discrimination activity can be found on page 14 to help the children learn about fruits and vegetables.

2. Read the book *Eating the Alphabet: Fruits & Vegetables from A to Z* by Lois Ehlert. Have the children identify all the fruits and vegetables pictured. Divide the children into groups and let them create their own fruit and vegetable alphabet books.

3. For a culminating activity, make vegetable soup. Send a note home to parents asking for donations of specific vegetables. A sample note for you to use can be found on page 13.

Sentence Strips

Use these sentence strips to review the story. Let the children work as partners or in small groups to complete the activities.

Activities

1. Enlarge and copy the sentence strips (below). Cut apart the strips and glue each one onto an oaktag sentence strip. Place the cards in scrambled order on a chalktray or in a pocket chart. Have the children arrange the cards in correct story order.

2. Make copies of the sentence strips below (one set per child or teams of two children). Glue each strip to the bottom of a separate sheet of paper. Have the children then illustrate the sentences and make big books.

3. Reproduce the sentence strips and cut them apart. Then cut apart the words on each sentence strip, taking care to keep each sentence strip's words separate. Glue each word onto half of a 5" x 8" (13 cm x 20 cm) index card. Place each mixed-up sentence in a pocket chart, chalktray, or on a flat surface. Direct the children to put the words in correct sentence order.

Sentences

We are going to grow vegetable soup.
Our tools are ready and we plant the vegetable seeds.
The sun and water help the vegetables grow.
We watch and weed the vegetables.
The vegetables are ready to be harvested.
We take the vegetables home and wash them.
The vegetables are cut up and put into a pot of water.
The vegetables cook into the best soup ever.

Language Experiences

On this page you will find a number of language experience ideas for you to use with your class. Modify and adapt the activities to suit your own classroom needs.

Recipes

After the class has cooked a batch of vegetable soup (any recipe will do), discuss how the vegetable soup was made. List the steps on chart paper. Direct the children to copy each step and draw a picture illustrating the steps. Just for fun, have the children write their own recipes for making vegetable soup. (Be ready for giggles as you read these creative versions!) Compile all the pages and make a class vegetable soup cookbook.

Alphabetical Order

You will need ten craft sticks, as well as red, orange, purple, green, and white tempera paint for this activity. Paint three craft sticks red; one craft stick orange; one craft sticks purple; four craft sticks green; one craft stick light green (mix a bit of white with the green tempera paint). After the craft sticks have dried, write a different vegetable name on each one matching color to correct vegetable name. Have the children work in small groups to alphabetize the words.

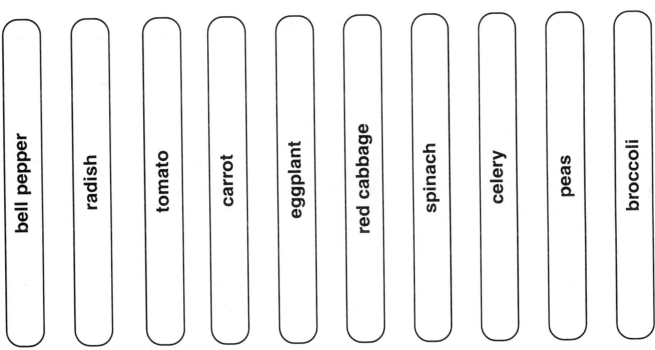

Extension: Cut out pictures of the vegetables and glue them to a piece of tagboard. Let the children match the words to the pictures.

Descriptions

Show the children that vegetables come in a variety of shapes. Pass a vegetable around so everyone can experience it. Ask the children to describe the shape of the vegetable. Examine a number of vegetables in the same manner. Give each child a sheet of white drawing paper and some crayons. Direct the children to draw the outline of any vegetable that they choose. Have them write some words (or draw pictures) inside the shape to describe the vegetable (descriptions may have to be written beyond its shape). Cut out and display the paper vegetables.

Vegetable Crafts

Here are two fun craft activities to introduce children to a wide variety of vegetables.

Vegetable Sculptures

Materials

raw vegetables (carrots, radishes, eggplant, potatoes, jicama, celery, zucchini, etc.); toothpicks; tiny marshmallows, raisins, pickles, olives, or other garnishes; whipped cream cheese; plastic knives

Directions

1. Choose one vegetable for the body. Cut up some of the other vegetables into chunks and pieces to use for body parts. Using the toothpicks, connect the vegetables to one another to make sculptures or funny faces (see diagram).

2. Add marshmallows, raisins, pickles, or other garnishes with a dollop of cream cheese. Let the children share their creations and have them identify by name the vegetables that were used in building their sculptures.

Vegetable Prints

Materials

newspaper; assorted vegetables (green pepper, corn on the cob, eggplant, etc.); kitchen knife; liquid tempera paint in a variety of colors; clean foam meat trays; white drawing or construction paper; one smock or old shirt for each child

Directions

1. Spread newspaper over your work surface. Pour a thin layer of each color of tempera paint into a separate foam meat tray. Cut each vegetable in half. (Make sure that each child is wearing a smock or cover-up before working with the paint.)

2. Instruct the children to pick up the uncut end of the vegetable and dip the cut end into a paint tray. Have the children press the painted end of the vegetable onto the sheet of drawing paper as many times as they would like, using more paint as necessary. Allow the prints to dry completely before displaying.

Vegetable Graphing

After sharing *Growing Vegetable Soup* with the class, let the children vote on their favorite vegetable from the story. Compile the information on a graph (see page 17, Extending the Book #3, for directions on making a reusable graph). Follow the procedure outlined below.

Materials

butcher paper; table; clear or masking tape; marking pens; yardstick; sticky notes or construction paper squares; crayons

Directions

1. Cut a piece of butcher paper large enough to cover a classroom table.

2. Use the yardstick as a guide to draw lines for a bar graph onto the butcher paper. You will need to make 11 rows, one for each vegetable named in the story. Make as many columns as you think you will need. Label each row with a different vegetable name. Tape the completed graph to the classroom table (see the partial graph at the bottom of this page).

Directions for the Children

1. Give each child a self-sticking note (or a construction paper square). Instruct the children to draw and color a picture of their favorite vegetable from the story.

2. Let the children place their notes on the graph one at a time (if using construction paper squares, tape them to the sections on the graph). Allow each child to explain his or her vegetable choice.

Follow Ups

Ask questions based on data obtained from the graph. For example:

1. Which vegetable is the favorite?

2. What is the difference between the number of votes for green beans and the number of votes for onions?

3. Which vegetables got the same number of votes?

4. How many votes are there altogether for the carrots and the potatoes?

Vegetable	Votes				
tomato					
green bean					
carrot					

Vegetable Treats

Cooking with vegetables is easy and if children have a hand in the preparation, they may be more eager for a taste.

Vegetable Soup

Look for some easy soup recipes in any of the cookbooks listed on page 76. Send a note home to enlist parent help to supply the vegetables and to supervise the preparation and cooking vegetable soup (a sample note home can be found on page 13). Before preparing soup, read aloud Marcia Brown's *Stone Soup*. Add a *washed* stone to soup pot; cook the soup.

Canned Plants

Sample some canned vegetables. Drain the water and cut the vegetables into small serving sizes. Place the vegetables into separate bowls. Provide a serving spoon for each bowl. Let the children place a bit of each vegetable onto their own paper plates. Discuss how the vegetables taste (sweet, sour, bitter, salty). Discuss how canned vegetables taste different than fresh vegetables. Brainstorm with the children why they think the canned vegetables taste different than the fresh ones. Learn about how we taste foods (see page 52).

Fancy Treats

Make some fancy garnishes with vegetables. You may want to enlist some adult volunteers to help in preparing these garnishes

Ingredients

carrots; celery; water; ice

Utensils

vegetable peeler; vegetable brush; knife; toothpicks; bowl

Directions

1. Review the safety rules (page 60).

2. Wash all the vegetables with a vegetable brush.

3. Peel the carrots with the vegetable peeler. Make paper-thin, length-wise slices from the carrots. Roll up each slice around your finger. Stick a toothpick through the curl to hold it together.

4. Cut each celery rib into short lengths. With a knife, make narrow slits in both ends of the celery piece. Soak the celery in ice water until the ends curl.

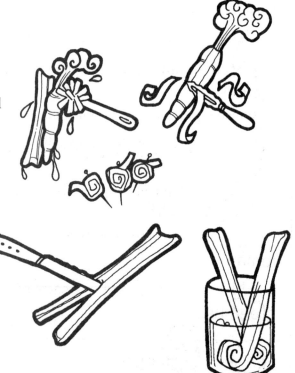

Correspondence

My Recipe

Dear Family,

_____is learning all
(Name)

about vegetables.

On_____our class will
(Day and Date)

be making vegetable soup. Please send the following

vegetable to school with your child on that day:

_____.

Please check one of the following statements:

_____   No, I will not be able to help the class on soup day.

_____   Yes, I will be able to help the class on soup day.

My phone number and name: _____

_____

Sign and return this letter by _____
                                                          date

Thank you for your cooperation.

Sincerely yours,

_____
Teacher Signature

Fruits and Vegetables

Some foods that we call vegetables are really fruits. Fruits have seeds. Tomatoes, zucchini, pumpkin, squash, and eggplant are actually fruits, not vegetables.

Color the fruits in the picture below.

Bread Bread Bread
by Ann Morris

Summary

Everybody in the world eats bread. Bread comes in all shapes and sizes from long, skinny loaves to round shapes with holes in the center. Bread is good for us because it helps our bodies grow strong. Breads are mixed and shaped, then baked, toasted, or cooked over a fire. People everywhere break bread together and enjoy this delicious, nutritious food.

The outline below is a suggested plan for using the various activities that are presented in this unit. You should adapt these ideas to fit your own classroom situation.

Sample Plan

Lesson 1

- Learn a Bread Chant (page 18).
- Compare breads; make a chart of the differences (page 18) using Fill Up Your Senses.
- Read *Bread Bread Bread*.
- Make peanut butter and jelly sandwiches; discuss the step-by-step procedure.
- Discuss the step-by-step procedure for growing wheat for bread using the Literature Connection found on page 20.

Lesson 2

- Write descriptive words (page 18).
- Play the mathematical Pizza Game (page 19).
- Make pizzas (page 61).
- Role-play action words (page 20).

Lesson 3

- Review *Bread Bread Bread*.
- Learn about Bread Around the World (page 22).
- Practice sequencing skills (page 21).
- Explore a different sort of bread: pancakes (page 24).

Lesson 4

- Make bread dough sculptures (page 23).
- Write bread rhymes (page 18).
- Explore pastabilities (page 57) after sharing that pasta is also from the bread group.
- How Many? Send home this following directions activity (page 26).

Lesson 5

- Explore other foods within the Bread Group (page 24).
- Read *Everybody Cooks Rice* by Norah Dooley (Carolrhoda, 1991). Learn to eat with chopsticks (page 25) and then try eating some cooked rice.
- Compare *Bread Bread Bread* with another bread story (see Bibliography on pages 79 and 80 for suggested titles).
- Create a bread collage (page 23).

Overview of Activities

Setting the Stage

1. Set up a bread display to include a variety of breads (bagels, pita, pizza slices, wheat bread, etc.). Have the children look through magazines to find pictures of these or other breads. Direct the children to cut out the pictures and match them to the real bread products.

2. Make peanut butter and jelly sandwiches. Discuss the step-by-step process. Tell the children that in order to make bread they must also follow a step-by-step procedure. Explore the process with the Literature Connection activities on page 20.

3. Read aloud some appropriate literature. Two fun books to share with the children are *Bread and Jam for Frances* by Russell Hoban and *Peanut Butter and Jelly* by Nadine Bernard Westcott.

4. Bake bread from scratch or use frozen dough or canned biscuits. Follow up with the sequencing activity on page 21.

Enjoying the Book

1. Show the children the pictures of bread in *Bread Bread Bread*. Ask the children to describe the breads. Record the words and have the children use the created word bank to write rhymes and fill in sentence frames (see page 18).

2. Engage the children in a math game. Pairs or small groups can play the Pizza Game (page 19).

3. Role-play some action words. Have one child enact an action while the rest of the group guesses the word. See helpful hints, Role Play, page 20.

4. Display a map of the world. Ask the children to identify some breads from around the world. On the map point out and flag the countries where the breads can be found.

Overview of Activities *(cont.)*

5. Make a batch of art bread dough (see recipe on page 23) for the children to use in making shapes.

6. Read *The Little Red Hen* by Paul Galdone. Follow up by making an *edible* bread recipe (page 23).

Extending the Book

1. Discuss and identify cereal, pasta, and rice that are a part of the Bread Group. Some activities for these foods include:

   • Use a variety of cereal shapes as math counters or for sorting experiences.

   • Make and eat pancakes.

   • Read a book about pancakes (see page 24) and have the children write their own pancake tale.

   • Sing "Yankee Doodle" and make a macaroni pasta dish.

   • Enjoy a variety of rice products, such as rice cakes or fried rice, and learn to eat with chopsticks (page 25).

   • Read *Strega Nona* by Tomie de Paola and make a big pot of pasta. Don't forget to say the chant as the pot is boiling.

   • Using dried pasta in a variety of shapes and sizes, have the children glue the pasta shapes on strong tagboard to form a collage. After glue dries, spray pasta collages with silver or gold spray paint. Allow to dry; display.

2. Assign page 26 for homework. Parents can help their children read the sentences.

3. Have the children vote for their favorite bread. Record the information on a graph. You may want to make a more permanent, reusable type of graph. To construct a reusable and portable graph, you will need a plain, plastic shower curtain, a permanent marking pen, a yardstick, and self-stick cup hooks. Use the marking pen to draw a grid (with rows and columns) with numerals in the first column. Mount four or more self-stick cup hooks at the top of the chalkboard. Suspend the graph. Tape paper labels as needed to the graph. Children can add information to the graph using self-sticking notes. (Wipe-off pens or construction paper pieces and tape may be used instead of the self-sticking notes.) To store, fold up the curtain.

Experiencing Bread

On this page you will find four different language experiences to use with the children pertaining to their bread experiences.

Fill Up Your Senses

Purchase a variety of breads (texture, color, density, etc.). A great resource is a day-old bread shop. Give each child one of the pieces of bread. Let them describe the physical attributes of the bread (color, shape, size, texture, smell, taste). Record their responses on chart paper; repeat with other breads. Use the words on the chart paper to write sentences about the breads. Have the children copy a sentence frame, like the one below, and fill in the blanks with words from the chart.

> ## My favorite breads are _____ and _____.

Descriptive Words

Ask the children to describe the shape of the breads they saw in *Bread Bread Bread*. Responses might include: long, skinny, fat, flat, holey, square, and round. Record their responses on chart paper. Use the created terminology in writing experiences or transferring the terminology to other items (i.e. *long* hallway, *short* chair, *holey* cheese, etc.)

Rhymes

After the descriptions list, above, has been completed, ask the children to name some rhyming words for each listed word. Write these rhyming words next to each word on the list (be aware the children may not be able to come up with a rhyming word for every descriptive word). Direct the children to use the words on this list to make up rhymes, for example:

> ### A *bagel* is *fat* and a *tortilla* is *flat*.
>
> ### *French bread* is *crunchy*, but *pretzels* are *munchy*.

Bread Chant

Teach the children this bread chant.

> **Red jam, purple jelly**
> **Yummy, yummy, in my belly.**
> **Take some bread—spread the jelly wide,**
> **Watch out tummy, it's coming inside.**
> **Spread it thick, say it quick,**
> **Spread it thicker, say it quicker!**

Keep repeating the chant and see how fast the children can say the words.

Pizza Game

Children will have fun seeing who can top their pizza first with this math game.

Materials

round paper plates (dinner size); black marking pens; scissors; business size envelopes; copies of the markers, below; manila envelopes

Directions

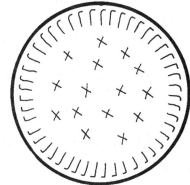

1. Prepare the paper plates by randomly drawing 15 large Xs on each one.
2. Make one copy of the markers, below, for each paper plate.
3. Cut out the markers, laminate, and store each set in a separate, labeled envelope. Place all the prepared paper plate pizzas and markers in a large manila envelope labeled: Pizza Game.

To Play

Two or more children can play this game. One die will be needed. Each player will need a paper plate pizza and a set of 15 markers. Tell the players to take turns rolling the die. After the first player rolls the die, he or she places the corresponding number of markers onto his or her pizza. Play continues in the same manner for each player. The first player to cover all the Xs on his or her pizza wins, but the players must roll the *exact* number to place the final pizza topping(s).

Markers

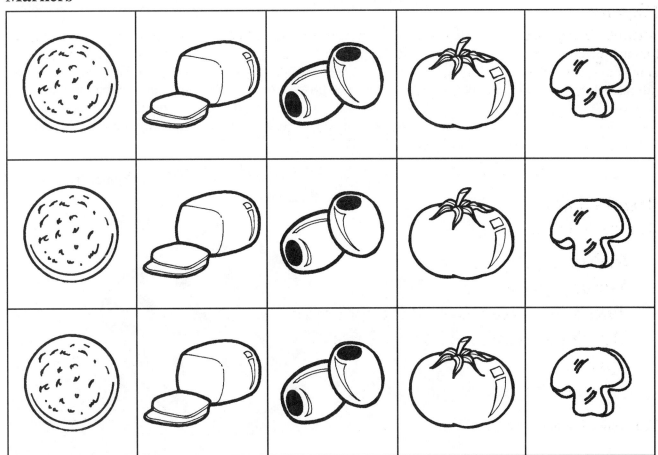

Step by Step

Whether you choose to make bread from scratch or you bake canned biscuits, the children will enjoy the end product. If a breadmaker is available for your use, take advantage of this timesaver. The activities on this page can be employed to introduce or extend the bread-making process.

Literature Connection

Introduce the bread-making process with a reading of *The Little Red Hen* by Paul Galdone. After you have read the story to the children, ask them to recall the materials that the red hen gathered in order to bake the bread. Display those same ingredients and show them to the children as you talk about them. Use the ingredients to bake bread following a chosen bread recipe. Follow up with the sequencing activity on page 21.

Recipes

After your class has baked bread, pair or group the children and have them write a bread-making recipe. First review the ingredients used and the step-by-step process used in making bread. List them on chart paper. Then allow the children to begin writing.

Role Play

Talk about the "ing" actions involved in making bread: measuring, mixing, kneading, shaping, baking, cooling, tasting, etc. Role-play these actions. Afterwards, sing a song using the tune of "Here We Go It Round the Mulberry Bush." Change the words in the first verse to, "This is the way we mix the bread . . ." The second verse could be, "This is the way we knead the bread . . ." Continue in the same manner for all the explored "-ing" action words.

Global Bread

Bread is a global food. People everywhere eat some form of bread. Show the children pictures of different types of bread such as bagels, pretzels, and tortillas. See if they can identify the breads and their countries of origin. Pin or tape each bread picture to its corresponding country on a world map. Use the Bread Around the World worksheet on page 22.

Extension: Ask the children to bring in a sample of the type(s) of breads they eat at home. This is especially exciting when you have a large multi-cultural classroom population.

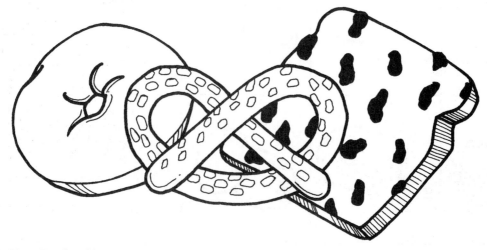

Making Bread

Reinforce sequencing skills with this activity.

Materials

one copy of the pictures (below) for each child; scissors; glue; long strips of construction paper

Directions

1. Give each child a copy of the pictures below, a long strip of construction paper, scissors, and glue.

2. Discuss the actions in the pictures with the children. Ask them to tell you which happens first, which happens next, etc.

3. Direct the children to cut out the squares and glue the pictures onto the construction paper strip in correct sequence. The children may number and color the pictures.

Bread Around the World

Find out about breads from around the world. Read the sentences. Cut and paste the pictures and put them into the correct boxes.

A **baguette** is a long, crusty bread that comes from **France**.

People in **Mexico** place meat and beans in the center of this flat, round **tortilla**.

German pretzels are rolled and twisted into a knot and sometimes covered with salt.

In **Africa**, the flat bread **injera** is used like a spoon to scoop up other foods.

Italians enjoy rectangular **focaccia** with seasonings on top.

In **Syria,** the way to enjoy a sandwich is with **pita bread**.

Artful Bread

Bread-making is an art, but you do not have to bake bread to be artistic. Already prepared bread can be used to create and inspire some very interesting art projects and activities. Three fun activities are described below.

Collage

Have a supply of magazines on hand. Instruct the children to look through them and find pictures of bread (including pancakes, waffles, muffins, etc.). Direct the children to cut them out and glue them to a sheet of tagboard. Assemble the finished tagboard illustrations and make a class collage; display.

Bread Dough

Materials

flour; salt; water; bowl; waxed paper; plastic wrap; 1-cup (240 mL) and ½-cup (120 mL) measuring cups; toothpicks; cookie sheet; oven; string, yarn, or thread

Directions

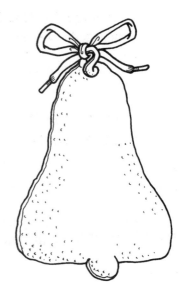

1. Measure and pour 4 cups (960 mL) of flour and 1 cup (240 mL) of salt into a bowl. Mix the ingredients by hand. Pour 1 cup (240 mL) of water into the center of the mixture and continue mixing by hand. Gradually add the remaining half cup (120 mL) of water to the mix.

2. Line a flat surface with sheets of waxed paper. (Note: If you slightly dampen the flat surface with water the waxed paper will stick better to surface and not move around while working with the dough.) Sprinkle some flour over the waxed paper. On this floured surface knead the dough until it is smooth.

3. Give each child a small ball of dough to make shapes. With a toothpick, make a hole completely through the dough in the top part of each shape. Place the shaped dough on cookie sheet and bake at 325 degrees Fahrenheit (160° C) for about one hour. Allow the shapes to cool thoroughly.

4. Push string, yarn, or thread through the hole in the shapes and hang them up as ornaments for display.

Note: These bread dough creations are for decoration only and not intended to be eaten.

Edible Dough

Thaw frozen bread dough to make shapes. After placing dough shapes on a baking sheet, decorate with raisins, cranberries, maraschino cherries, nuts, etc. Bake as directed. Enjoy the yummy edible bread treats.

Beyond Bread

Explore some other foods within the bread group—pasta, pancakes, cereals, and rice—with any of these activities.

Pasta

1. Sing "Yankee Doodle" or read aloud *Strega Nona* by Tomie de Paola (Prentice Hall, 1975). Enjoy spaghetti for lunch or as a snack.

2. Give each group of children several different lengths of dry pasta. Direct the children to arrange the pasta according to size from smallest to largest. Let them glue their pasta to strips of construction paper to make pasta charts (see diagram).

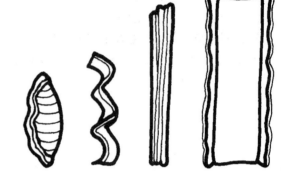

Pancakes

1. Share *Pancakes for Breakfast* by Tomie de Paola (Harcourt Brace Jovanovich, 1978) with the class. Have them write the story in their own words.

2. Read some other pancake stories: *Latkes and Applesauce: A Hanukkah Story* by Fran Manushkin, and *Pancakes, Pancakes!* by Eric Carle.

3. Sing a pancake song to the first four lines from the tune "I'm a Little Teapot."

   I'm a little pancake, round and thick
   I'm good with syrup–sure makes it stick.

   I'm a little pancake, soft and flat
   I'm fun to nibble–and that's a fact.

Cereal

Mix a variety of cereals together, such as alphabet shapes, animal shapes, spheres, and ohs. Provide each child with a cupful of the mix. Instruct them to sort the cereal according to color, shape, or size. Then use the cereal shapes as math counters.

Rice Is Nice

1. Learn about rice dishes and products in different parts of the world. Read *Everybody Cooks Rice* by Norah Dooley.

2. Sample a variety of rice dishes. Teach the children how to eat rice with chopsticks (see page 25 for instructions). You may want to ask a local Asian restaurant if they would like to donate chopsticks for your class' use. If there is not a restaurant available, chopsticks can be purchased at most cooking supply stores.

Eating with Chopsticks

1. Rest one chopstick between the thumb and forefinger of your right hand (or left hand if you are left-handed). The lower half of the chopstick should rest against your ring finger.

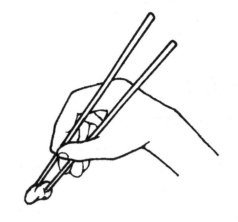

2. Hold the second chopstick like you would hold a pencil or a crayon. Hold the chopstick between your thumb and forefinger.

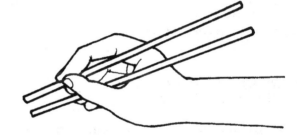

3. Keep the first chopstick still. Move the second chopstick up and down to pick up food. Don't be upset if it is hard to do at first. It takes lots of practice!

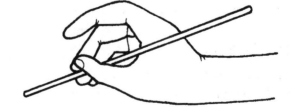

Practice picking up cotton balls, paper clips, or other small items with chopsticks before you try to eat food with your chopsticks

How Many?

Read the directions in each section with your child. Have him or her complete the drawing. Let your child count the objects in the picture and write the number in the small box.

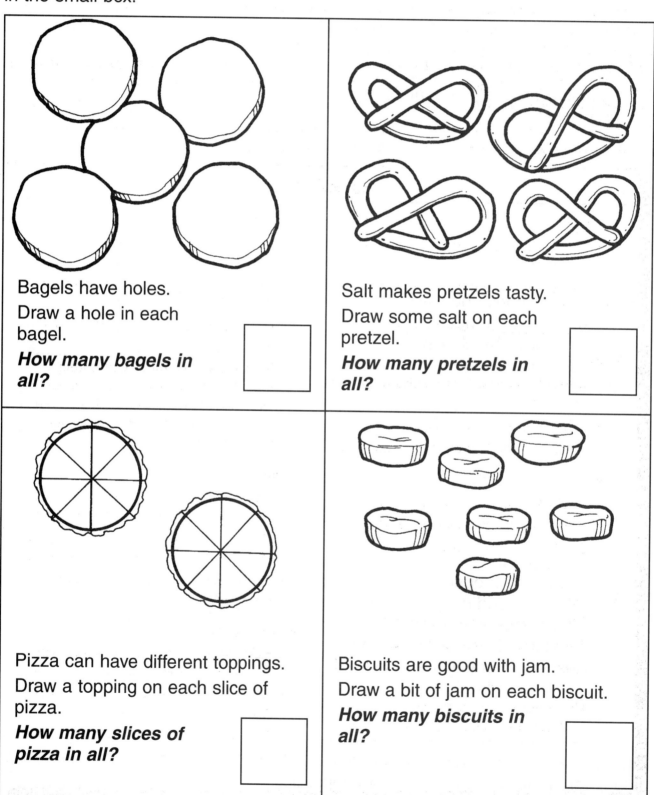

Bagels have holes.
Draw a hole in each bagel.
How many bagels in all?

Salt makes pretzels tasty.
Draw some salt on each pretzel.
How many pretzels in all?

Pizza can have different toppings.
Draw a topping on each slice of pizza.
How many slices of pizza in all?

Biscuits are good with jam.
Draw a bit of jam on each biscuit.
How many biscuits in all?

Gregory the Terrible Eater
by Mitchell Sharmat

Summary

Gregory, a young goat, was a terrible eater. Instead of tin cans, pieces of rug, or other goat food, Gregory preferred fruits and vegetables. Worried about his health, Gregory's parents took him to the doctor. After speaking with Gregory, Dr. Ram assured Gregory's parents that all would be well. He told them that picky eaters have to develop a taste for good food slowly. That night Mother Goat prepared a new meal—spaghetti and a shoelace in tomato sauce. Soon Gregory was eating everything. In fact, he began eating too much. Once again his parents intervened. This time they let him eat all of the junk food he wanted. After going to bed with a terrible stomach ache, Gregory woke up and ordered a sensible breakfast.

The outline below is a suggested plan for using the various activities that are presented in this unit. You should adapt these ideas to fit your own classroom situation.

Sample Plan

Lesson 1

- Discuss junk food (page 28, Setting The Stage, #2).
- Learn a food chant (page 28, Setting The Stage, #3).
- Read *Gregory the Terrible Eater.*

Lesson 2

- Retell the story with flannelboard puppets (page 30).
- Draw Gregory's meal (page 31).
- Make Fold-out Food Pyramids (page 35).

Lesson 3

- Begin writing a Food Diary (page 34).
- Choose nutritious foods (page 32).
- Read some poems about food (pages 45 and 46).

Lesson 4

- Work on Food Diaries (page 34).
- Make some Edible Jewelry (page 58).
- Homework: Learn about nutrients found in food (page 36).
- Use some more of the Poetry Connections (pages 45 and 46).

Lesson 5

- Complete the Food Diaries.
- Write an innovation of *Gregory the Terrible Eater* (page 29, Extending the Book, #2).
- Learn about the dangers of junk food (page 37).
- Review the need for healthy eating. Provide each child with an assembled *My Food Book* (pages 42–44). Read the first page and allow children to create an illustration and color it.

Lesson 6

- Choose from the fruit activities on page 38 to teach more about this food group.
- Choose from the eggs activities on page 39 to teach more about this food group.
- Complete pages 2 and 3 of *My Food Book.*

Lesson 7

- Enjoy some of the milk–group activities found on pages 40 and 41.
- Complete pages 4 and 5 of the *My Food Books.*
- Reread *Gregory the Terrible Eater* and culminate with a discussion on what "healthy eating" means.

Overview of Activities

Setting the Stage

1. Set up a Dramatic Play Center with a child-size stove and refrigerator, plastic food, cooking utensils, table and chairs, and aprons. Add some shelves, paper grocery bags, and a cash register. Ask families to send empty cereal boxes and other food containers; add them to the center. Have the children role-play working and shopping in a grocery store and preparing a meal with the props available.

2. Bring in packages and wrappers from junk food and show them to the class. Ask the children to define junk food. Discuss why junk food isn't good for them and have them tell you what foods would be better for snacks (see page 37 for a prepared activity). Serve a healthy snack, such as sliced, fresh fruits or vegetables.

3. Recite this chant with the children:

> **Chocolate on my pancakes,**
> **Chocolate on my peas,**
> **Chocolate in my milk,**
> **Pass the syrup, please.**
> **Too much chocolate in me—now my stomach aches, ow-y!**

Let them invent words for a new "junk food" chant.

Enjoying the Book

1. Retell the story of Gregory using the story props on page 30. Use the patterns as flannel board pieces or attach each prop to a craft stick to use as puppets.

2. Ask the children to name some of the foods that Gregory liked to eat. Let the children make a meal for Gregory. See page 31 for a prepared activity.

3. Have the children draw pictures of a healthy meal on paper plates or let them cut out pictures from magazines to paste onto the plates.

4. Maybe Gregory had a difficult time deciding on what actually tasted good. Complete the How We Taste Foods activity on page 52.

5. Gregory was a young goat. As most "kids" like to do, he loved to play. Complete some of the Let's Get Physical activities found on page 62.

Overview of Activities *(cont.)*

Enjoying the Book *(cont.)*

6. Make tagboard or construction paper strips. Write a sentence on each for the children to finish (see below). Place the strips at your classroom Writing Center to use during planned or free time use.

> # My favorite food is _____.

7. For easy reference to remind them of different foods in each food group, have the children make Fold-out Food Pyramids (page 35). Instruct the children to keep a record of what they have eaten for each meal by writing (or drawing a picture) about it in the corresponding food group.

Extending the Book

1. Tell the children that different foods have different nutrients. A body needs a variety of nutrients to keep fit. Learn about these nutrients. Assign page 36 for homework. (**Note:** Page 36 will give you the background information for your explanation on nutrients.)

2. Write an innovation of *Gregory the Terrible Eater*. Change the title to *Gregory the Wonderful Eater*. Ask children to name other parts of the story that would have to change to fit with the new title (see the chart below for an example).

Gregory the Terrible Eater	Gregory the Wonderful Eater
Gregory the Terrible Eater liked to eat vegetables and fruits. His parents wanted him to eat tin cans, boxes, and _____.	Gregory the Wonderful Eater liked to eat _____ and _____. His parents wanted him to eat _____.

3. Human parents may think that Gregory was a wonderful eater. After all, he liked eating fruits and vegetables. But he also ate too much junk food. Learn why junk food is not good for the body. See page 37 for a prepared activity.

4. Since Gregory loved to nibble his food, have the children make Edible Jewelry (page 58) that they can wear and nibble on throughout the day.

Story Props

Copy, color, and cut out these *Gregory the Terrible Eater* story props. Laminate and trim them. Glue a piece of felt to the back of each piece to use on a flannel board or staple a craft stick to each piece and use as stick puppet props.

Making Gregory's Meal

Make a meal for Gregory. Color the pictures of some things that you think Gregory would like to eat. Cut them out and paste them onto the dish.

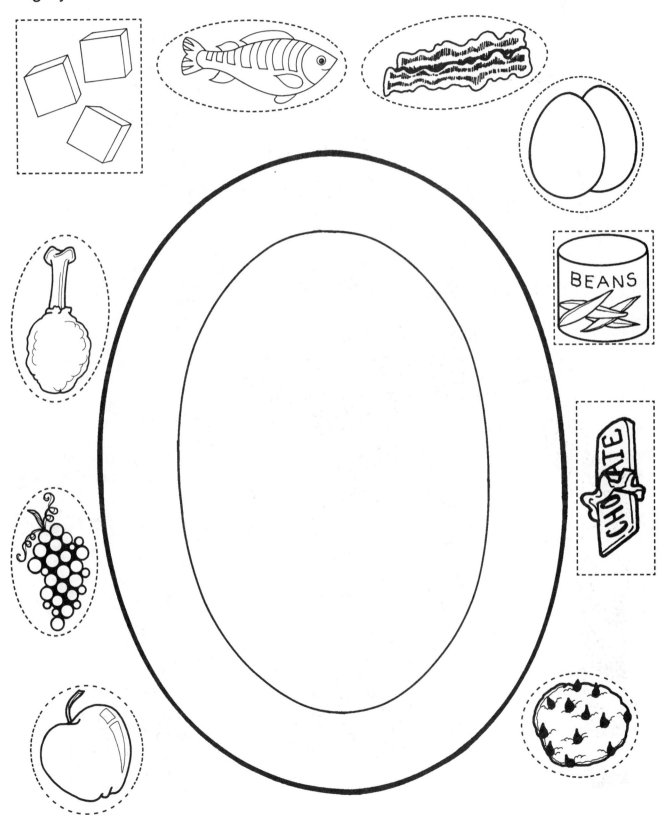

Making Gregory's Meal *(cont.)*

After the children have made a meal for Gregory (page 31), follow up with any of the activities on this page.

Writing

Have the children write a sentence about the meal they made for Gregory. Let them read it to a partner or have them share it with the whole group.

> ## Gregory likes to eat _____, _____, and _____.

Nutritious Meals

Give each child a paper plate and some crayons. Direct the children to draw pictures of some foods that would make a good, nutritious breakfast, lunch, or dinner. (If preferred, let the children cut out food pictures from magazines; glue them to the plates.) Identify the food groups that are represented on each plate. Keep a Food Pyramid chart on hand (page 67) or let the children make fold-out food pyramids for easy reference (page 35).

More Nutritious Meals

Have the children keep a food diary for a period of time. See pages 33 and 34 for directions and a data collection form to use. Enlist help from the children's families in recording what the children ate at each meal. Have the children share their food diaries upon completion.

Foods

Have the children look through magazines for pictures of foods and other items. Direct the children to cut out a picture. One at a time, let the children explain why they think Gregory would like to eat that item. Ask the children if Gregory's parents would approve of that food; why or why not? Ask the children if their parents would approve of that food; why or why not?

Food Diary

In order to help your children become healthy eaters, they must have an idea of what constitutes a healthy diet. A food diary is one tool that will visually aid children in determining whether or not they are eating a healthy variety of foods. Have the children keep a food diary for a period of time from one day to one week. Make copies of page 34 for them to complete. Introduce and reinforce your lessons with any of the following ideas.

Food Pyramid

Before beginning this activity you may want to review the food pyramid with the children. Display a poster or bulletin board (see pages 69–75) that features the food pyramid. Reread the five food groups with the children. Discuss how many servings of each food are needed daily. Keep a food pyramid on display throughout this lesson.

Choices

Give each child one or more copies of the food diary page (page 34). Show the class how to complete the sections. Depending on their skill level, children may write words or draw pictures about their food choices. After the allotted time is over, discuss the food pages with the children. Ask them if they ate the recommended number of fruits and vegetables that day. Continue questioning about the other food groups. If they ate a food from each food group in one day, have those children make a pyramid with their hands (see diagram at right).

Class Chart

Collect all the data gathered during the Choices activity (above) to make a class chart. With the class read the chart and ask these questions:

- From which food group did they eat the most foods?

- From which food group did they eat the least foods?

- What is the whole class's favorite food group?

What Have You Been Eating?

If you think the children can handle a "research project," have them provide a Food Diary packet (five days worth of page 34) to a family member who will track his/her personal eating for five days. When the packet is returned the children will then evaluate if the family member has been eating "junky" or healthy.

Food Diary *(cont.)*

Name _____ Day _____ Date _____

Today I ate foods from these groups:

Bread, Cereal, Rice, and Pasta

Fruit

Vegetable

Milk, Yogurt, and Cheese

Meat, Poultry, Fish, Beans, Eggs, and Nuts

Fats, Oils, and Sweets

Fold-Out Food Pyramid

Fold-out food pyramids are certainly eye-catching and unusual. Plus, they are easy to make. Just follow the directions below.

Materials

white construction paper cut into 12" (30 cm) squares; scissors; clear plastic tape; crayons or colored marking pens

Directions

1. Fold the square in half diagonally to make a triangle.

2. Fold the triangle in half; then open up to a square shape again.

3. Cut apart the four triangles on the creased lines.

4. Place the sections side by side and tape together using this sequential format: tape b to c; and c to d; and d to a.

5. Label the left upper triangle Vegetable Group; lower left triangle Fruit Group; lower right triangle Bread Group; upper right triangle Oils & Fats.

6. Fold down the upper left triangle. Label it Meat Group.

7. Fold the triangular flap towards the right. Label it Milk Group.

8. Fold the bottom section up. Label it The Food Pyramid. Reopen (backwards) one triangle at a time to slowly reveal the food pyramid. Have the children draw appropriate pictures in each section.

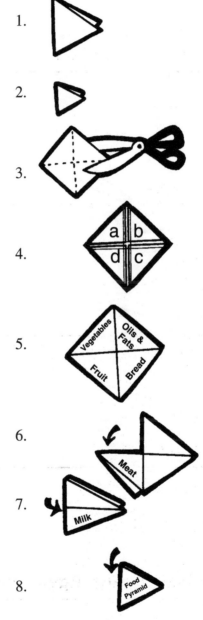

Note: If preferred, you can make one large food pyramid for the whole class. Use large sheets of tagboard or construction paper to make the triangular segments. Have the children look through magazines for pictures to cut out and paste on the triangular pages. Tape the sections together in the same manner as described above.

How Food Helps You

Read this page with your child. Ask your child to identify the foods pictured. Let them color the pictures.

Different foods have different nutrients that help you keep fit.

Foods from the **Bread Group** have **carbohydrates**. Carbohydrates give you energy.

Foods from the **Fruit and Vegetable Groups** have **Vitamins C and A**. These vitamins help you see in the dark, help heal cuts, and help keep you well.

Foods from the **Milk Group** have **calcium**. Calcium makes bones grow strong.

Foods from the **Meat Group** have **protein**. Protein helps muscles grow.

Foods from the **Fats and Oils Group** do not contain as many nutrients as the foods in the other five groups.

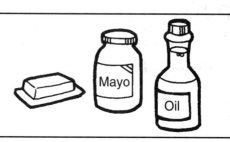

Too Much Junk Food!

After Gregory ate too much junk food he got a stomach ache. When you eat too much junk food you can get more than a stomach ache. Junk food can make your body feel awful and you can even gain weight that you might not want to gain.

What is junk food? Junk food is any food that has lots of sugar and salt in them instead of nutrients. Potato chips, packaged desserts, and sugar-coated cereals are junk food. Too much sugar and salt can cause you to feel tired or give you headaches. Even worse, too much sugar and salt can make you fat.

Look at the food pictures below. Some of them show pictures of junk food. Put an X through the junk food pictures. Color the foods that are good for you.

Completing the Food Pyramid

Not all of the five food groups have been discussed in-depth in this book. To complete the Food Pyramid, use the following activities and projects to introduce and explore the Fruit Group, Meat Group, and Milk Group. Culminate this section with the *My Food Book* on pages 42 to 44 or use the pages as you move through the additional food groups. (Make copies of the pages for each child. Cut out the pages on the dashed lines and staple them together along one edge. Read the text with the children and let them color the pictures.) **Note:** Before feeding the children, make sure no one is allergic to any of the food items being sampled.

Fruit

Fruit provides the body with important nutrients and is a key source of fiber. It is recommended that two to four servings of fruit be eaten every day. Teach children about fruit with the following activities.

Seeds

1. Most fruits have seeds. Compare the seeds of different fruits. How are they alike? How are they different?

2. Before cutting open a fruit, estimate how many seeds will be inside. After cutting it open count the seeds.

3. Roast pumpkin seeds. Cut open a pumpkin and scoop out the seeds. Remove pulp from the seeds. Spread some cleaned pumpkin seeds on a cookie sheet and sprinkle with salt. Bake at 350 degrees Fahrenheit (180 degrees C) for about 30 minutes, shaking the cookie sheet every ten minutes. For the best flavor, do not let the seeds turn brown.

4. If you have not completed the Fruits and Vegetables activity on page 14, do so now.

Cooking with Fruit

Fruit is delicious by itself, but combined with other fruits it can be transformed into a tastier and fancy treat. Thread cut fruit chunks onto wooden skewers to make Fruit Kabobs (page 63) or make easy parfaits by combining berries with plain yogurt in tall plastic glasses. Top parfaits with dollops of whipped cream.

Literature

Enjoy some books about fruit: *Eating the Alphabet. Fruits & Vegetables from A to Z* by Lois Ehlert ; *Apples and Pumpkins* by Anne Rockwell; *The Carrot Seed* by Ruth Krauss; *Johnny Appleseed* by Reeve Lindbergh.

Eggsciting Activities

Eggs

Eggs are part of the Meat, Poultry, Fish, Dry Beans, and Nuts Group. We need to eat two to three servings from this group every day. Learn more about eggs with these fun food activities.

Hatching

Hatch fertilized eggs in the classroom. For information and how-tos, contact your local Agricultural Extension Agency. Learn how eggs hatch by sharing some books with the class: *The Egg: A First Discovery Book* by Gallimard Jeunesse and Pascale de Bourgoing (Scholastic, Inc., 1997) and *Egg: A Photographic Story of Hatching* by Robert Burton (Dorling Kindersley, 1997).

Note: Be certain you discuss the difference between a fertilized egg (has a baby chick in it) and an eating egg (no baby chick in it). If you do not, the children may think that the eggs at home, or the ones used in the next activity listed on this page, have babies in them. They will become quite disturbed when you crack open the eggs and cook them!

Inside the Egg

Crack open an egg and examine it. Name all the parts. Scramble some eggs and cook them for a tasty treat.

Tissue Eggs

Create some unusual designs with art tissue eggs. First, cut out an egg shape from white construction paper. Cut colored art tissue into a variety of shapes and sizes that will fit onto the white construction paper egg. Paint the surface of the white cutout completely with vinegar and then place the tissue paper pieces on the wet surface. Let the cutouts dry completely. The tissue paper pieces will fall away (or remove gently) to reveal some interesting designs; display.

Nuts

Nuts are also included in the Meat Food Group. Crack open walnuts, almonds, and pecans. Use the removed shells to make a collage by gluing nut shells onto cardboard to make a design. Paint the shells with tempera colors. Use the nut meats over ice cream or in a baked treat.

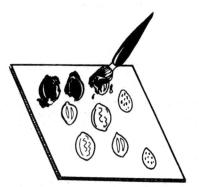

Peanuts

Make homemade peanut butter. Place two cups (480 mL) of shelled peanuts (save the shells to make a collage, see above) in a food processor or blender. Blend for six to ten minutes until a paste is formed. Scoop out paste; serve on crackers or slices of bread.

Dairy Products

Milk, Yogurt, and Cheese

According to the food pyramid, two to three servings of milk, yogurt, and cheese are needed daily. These food products contain calcium which makes bones and teeth strong. Explore these foods with the following projects.

Milk

Field Trip

Visit a local dairy farm or read Aliki's *From Cow to Carton*. Sample some milk products. Record pre-post taste thoughts. Explain that our tastes are our opinion. At snack time, drink chocolate milk or make milk shakes.

Milk Paint

Prepare a batch of milk paint. For each color desired you will need two tablespoons (30 mL) of nonfat milk powder and enough water to make a thick, smooth paste. Add a few drops of food coloring; mix well. Let the children paint pictures on white drawing paper with standard art brushes.

Cottage Cheese			
Before I tasted it		After I tasted it	
☺ ☺ ☺	☹ ☹ ☹	☺ ☺ ☺	☹ ☹ ☹
☺ ☺	☹ ☹ ☹	☺ ☺ ☺	☹ ☹ ☹
	☹ ☹ ☹	☺ ☺ ☺	☹ ☹ ☹
	☹ ☹ ☹	☺ ☺	
	☹ ☹ ☹		

Yogurt

Homemade Yogurt

Make some yogurt using a commercial yogurt maker. Sample the finished product. Add some fresh fruit, granola, and a bit of honey to sweeten the taste. If a commercial yogurt maker is not available, taste some prepared yogurt. (Save and clean the yogurt cups to use in the classroom as sorting containers, sand molds, musical instruments, or paint containers.) Make pre-post opinion graphs for the different flavors of yogurt sampled.

Cheese

Tasty Treats

Sample a variety of cheeses (don't forget the pre-post opinion graphs). Then make some easy cheese roll-ups: Place a thin slice of luncheon meat on a thin slice of cheese and roll up for an instant sandwich.

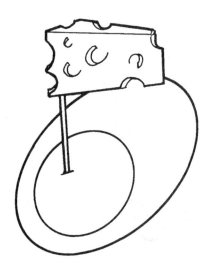

Another tasty treat is to make cheese boat snacks. Cook hardboiled eggs and slice them in half. Attach a triangular piece of cheese to each egg half with a toothpick so it resembles a sail.

Sing "The Farmer in the Dell" which ends with ". . . the cheese stands alone."

From Cow to You

Milk comes from cows. Milk has protein, vitamins, and minerals that give you energy and make you strong. Many foods are made from milk. Find the names of some foods made from milk in the word search puzzle. The pictures are clues to help you find the six hidden milk products.

c	l	c	c	h	e	e	s	e
o	i	e	b	f	g	m	z	l
t	c	x	u	c	e	k	l	m
t	e	p	t	r	j	q	b	l
a	c	b	t	i	c	m	u	b
g	r	r	e	b	j	e	t	k
e	e	o	r	o	d	i	z	s
c	a	t	m	u	a	z	e	o
h	m	e	y	o	g	u	r	t
e	c	f	l	e	t	g	m	e
e	o	s	v	f	n	w	i	s
s	n	m	a	b	l	g	l	p
e	e	u	s	y	e	x	k	e

My Food Book
by

_____

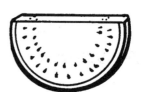

Start the day with a bowl of cereal and some milk,
a glass of orange juice, and a slice of toast.

1

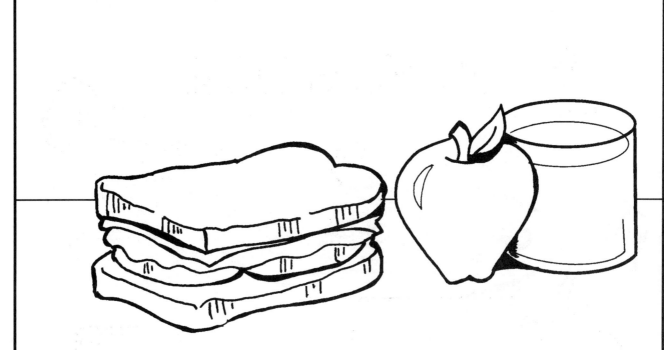

A sandwich, some fruit, and a glass of milk make a good lunch.

2

Cottage Cheese

Snack on a piece of fruit or some cottage cheese and crackers.

3

Time for dinner! Eat some fish, salad, and vegetables.

4

For dessert, have fruit salad or fruit topped with yogurt.

5

Poetry Connections

There are numerous poems and rhymes available to use with your food and nutrition unit. Listed on this page and the next are some suggested titles and resources.

Mother Goose

Browse through any collection of Mother Goose rhymes and you will find such all-time favorites as "Peter Peter Pumpkin Eater," "Little Miss Muffet," "Sing a Song of Sixpence," and "Pat-a-Cake." Recite them and create hand movements for each one. A collection of additional poems are listed on page 46.

Poems and Rhymes

Veggie Poetry

Recite this poem with the children. Then give them a chance to change the poem by naming another vegetable. Be sure they change the color words to match their chosen vegetable.

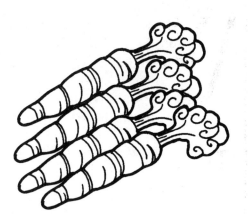

Way down in the garden, two orange carrots sat.
Growing, growing, growing until they were fat.

Variation:

Way down in the garden, three red tomatoes sat.
Growing, growing, growing until they were fat.

Pasta Tune

Sing this song to the tune of "Twinkle, Twinkle, Little Star."

Boil, boil little pot, make the pasta very hot.
Cook it slowly, cook it quick.
Either way won't make it stick.
Boil, boil little pot, make the pasta very hot.

Cook some pasta. Drain it and toss with some butter and Parmesan cheese. Yum!

Unrhymes

Let the children fill in the blank in this verse with a food name. It won't rhyme, but that's the fun of it. Repeat using other food names.

Mom gave me some money to buy some honey.
But I didn't buy honey. I bought some _____.

Mom gave me a nickel to buy a pickle.
But I didn't buy a pickle. I bought a _____.

Mom gave me a dime to buy a lime.
But I didn't buy a lime. I bought a _____.

Poetry Connections *(cont.)*

Poetry Collections

You may want to include some of these poetry collections in your food unit. Check your school or local library for these titles. Preview each book to find those poems that are most suitable for your class.

The Earth Is Painted Green. edited by Barbara Brenner (Scholastic, Inc., 1994).

> **"The Corn Grows Up"** by Navajo Indians
> **"The Man in the Onion Bed"** by John Ciardi
> **"Mushrooms Are Umbrellas"** by Arnold Spilka
> **"Oh! I Ate Them All"** by Shiki
> **"Pumpkin"** by Valerie Worth

Eats. by Arnold Adoff (Lothrop, Lee & Shepard Books, 1979). All the poems in this book are food-related.

Knees of a Natural Man: The Selected Poetry of Henry Dumas. (Thunder's Mouth Press, 1989).

> **"Peas"**

Poems for the Very Young. selected by Michael Rosen (Kingfisher Books, 1993).

> **"Chocolate Milkshake"** by Tania Mead
> **"Grandad's Dinners"** by Joan Poulson
> **"Tippety, Tippety Tin"** (anonymous)
> **"Hot Dogs Forever"** by Sonja Dunn
> **"If You're No Good at Cooking"** by Kit Wright
> **"Spaghetti! Spaghetti!"** by Jack Prelutsky

Poem Stew. by William Cole (Lippincott, 1981).

> **"Rhinoceros Stew"** by Mildred Luton
> **"Vegetables"** by Shel Silverstein

Rain Makes Applesauce. by Julian Scheer and Marvin Bileck (Holiday House, 1964).

Ride a Purple Pelican. by Jack Prelutsky (Greenwillow Books, 1986).

> **"Poor Potatoes"**
> **"Betty Ate a Butternut"**

Tasty Poems. collected by Jill Bennett (Oxford University Press, 1992).

> **"Oodles of Noodles"** by Lucia and James C. Hymes, Jr.

Vacation Time. by Nikki Giovanni (William Morrow and Company, 1980).

> **"The Reason I Like Chocolate"**

Food Riddles

Can you guess the answers to these riddles? Color the pictures in each row that fit the clues.

1. What foods are called vegetables but are really fruits?

2. What foods can grow without seeing the sun?

3. What foods hide inside a hard shell?

4. What foods can swim in water?

5. What foods hide many seeds inside?

6. What foods are grasses?

A Garden Plan

Growing a garden will take some time and planning, but it will be well worth the effort. On this page you will find a helpful outline of the steps you will need to take to prepare your garden.

The Plan

1. Write a list of all the vegetables that you want to grow. Check with a local nursery to determine which vegetables grow well in your area, as well as what time of year should the seeds/seedlings need to be planted.

2. Draw a map showing where you will put each type of vegetable plant.

3. Choose your garden site. It should be a sunny spot, away from large trees, but close to a source of water. If a garden site is not available you can grow your plants in a portable garden (see page 49 for plans).

4. Outline the garden area with rope and wood stakes. Use a shovel to dig about 8 inches (20 cm) into the ground. Add fertilizer, animal manure, or compost. Wait about four weeks or more before planting.

5. In the meantime, grow the seedlings indoors. For some suggested methods, see the page 49.

6. Make labels for each type of seed. Cut out construction paper squares and cut two slits in each. Write the name of the vegetable on each square label. Thread the head of a plastic spoon through the slits (see diagram). Make sure that the paper fits over the spoon; adjust the slits if necessary. Cover the head of the spoon with a plastic bag and seal it with a tie or rubber band.

7. When it is time, dig the garden topsoil into crumbly particles. Plant and label the seeds/seedlings using your pre-made map as a guide.

Timeline

Dig the garden bed; add compost.

Decide on what to plant; gather the seeds.

Plant the seeds in egg carton cups; make labels for the plants.

Re-dig the soil; plant the seeds and/or seedlings and label them. Water when the soil feels dry.

Week 1   **Week 2**   **Week 3**   **Week 4**

A Garden Plan *(cont.)*

Planting Seeds

Materials

cardboard egg cartons, yogurt cups, or other small containers; nail or scissors; clean foam meat trays; potting soil; craft sticks or plastic spoons; seeds; plastic bags and ties; water

Directions

1. With a nail or scissors, make a few drainage holes in the bottom of the egg cartons or plastic containers.

2. Fill the egg carton cups or other containers about ³/₄ full with soil. With a craft stick or plastic spoon, make a small hole in the center of each egg container.

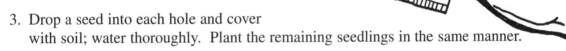

3. Drop a seed into each hole and cover with soil; water thoroughly. Plant the remaining seedlings in the same manner.

4. Wrap each container in a plastic bag; close the top and tie. Place the containers on foam meat trays and put them in a warm, dark place. After the seeds have sprouted, remove the bags. Place the seedlings in a sunny spot or under grow lights (see Resources on page 78 for possible purchasing sources).

5. The seedling still in its cardboard egg carton cup, may be planted in the garden when it is time. Other seedlings will have to be removed from their plastic containers before planting.

6. Reproduce the Plant Record on page 50 for the children to record their garden-growing observations.

Portable Gardens

Make a portable garden. Materials are in **bold** print.

1. With a **utility knife**, trim the sides of a **heavy, cardboard box** to a height of 6 inches (15 cm). Line the inside of the box with a **plastic garbage bag** cut to fit. Add a layer of **stones** or **pebbles** to completely cover the plastic bottom.

2. Pour **potting soil** into the box. With a **spoon** or your hand make small holes for the **seeds, seedlings,** or **small mature plants**. Plant the seeds, seedlings, or small plants in the holes. Cover with soil and **water**. Check the soil daily; water when soil feels dry.

3. Transport the box to a sunny spot, preferably outdoors. Observe growth changes over a period of time. Reproduce the Plant Record (page 50) for the children to record their observations.

Plant Record

Today is _____. I checked my plant. This is how it looked:	Today is _____. I checked my plant. This is how it looked:
Today is _____. I checked my plant. This is how it looked:	Today is _____. I checked my plant. This is how it looked:

The Food Chain

Learn about the food chain. Cut out the pictures below. Paste them onto a sheet of construction paper. Color the pictures.

1. Decomposers turn waste into "food" for plants.

2. Green plants use food from the ground to grow.

3. Plant eaters eat plants. Then they become food for meat eaters.

4. Meat eaters make waste for the decomposers to use.

How We Taste Foods

Did you know that different parts of your tongue can taste different flavors? On your tongue you have bumps or taste buds that let you taste bitter, sour, salty, and sweet foods. The picture of the tongue below shows you where you taste bitter, sour, salty, and sweet foods. Draw a line from the pictures at the bottom of the page to the part of the tongue where they will be tasted. Color the pictures. Circle your favorite taste.

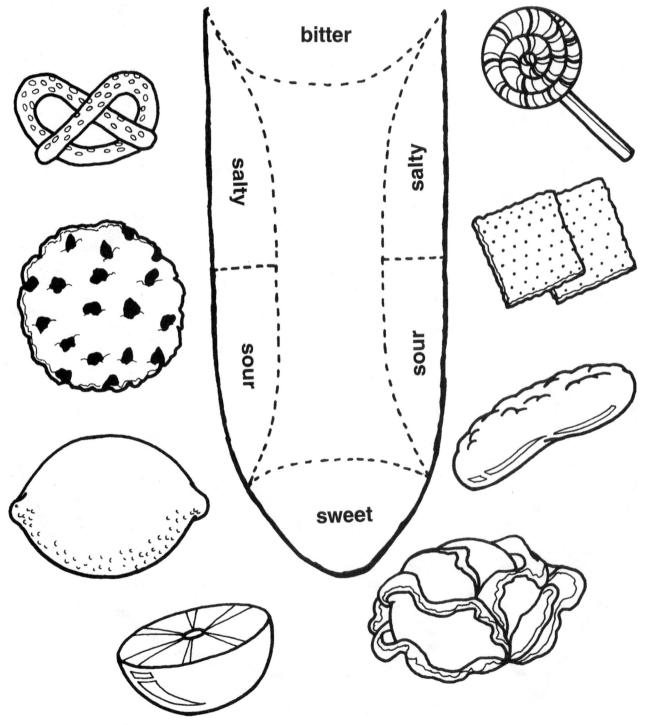

Water

Water is an important nutrient. Your body is made up mostly of water. Without water to drink, you would die. Water helps your body break down food for digestion and keeps your body from getting too warm. You get some water from the fruits and vegetables that you eat. Milk and juices also contains some of the water that you need. But you still need to drink eight glasses of water every day. Look at the drop of water below. How many times can you count the word water?

I counted water ☐ times.

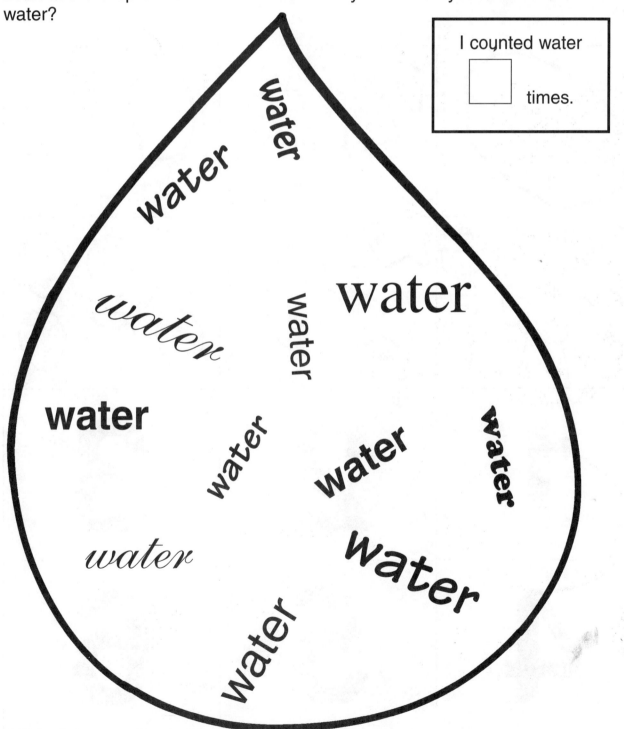

Food Match

Make a food matching game for the children to play individually or with a partner. Copy, color, and cut out the squares below. Glue them to tagboard or construction paper and laminate for durability. Store the squares in a marked manila envelope. Direct the children to count the pictures and match the correct numeral to the number of food items in each picture.

Note: To make the game self-correcting, write the corresponding numeral on the back of each picture. To extend game to larger numbers, have the children make the numbers and corresponding food sets themselves.

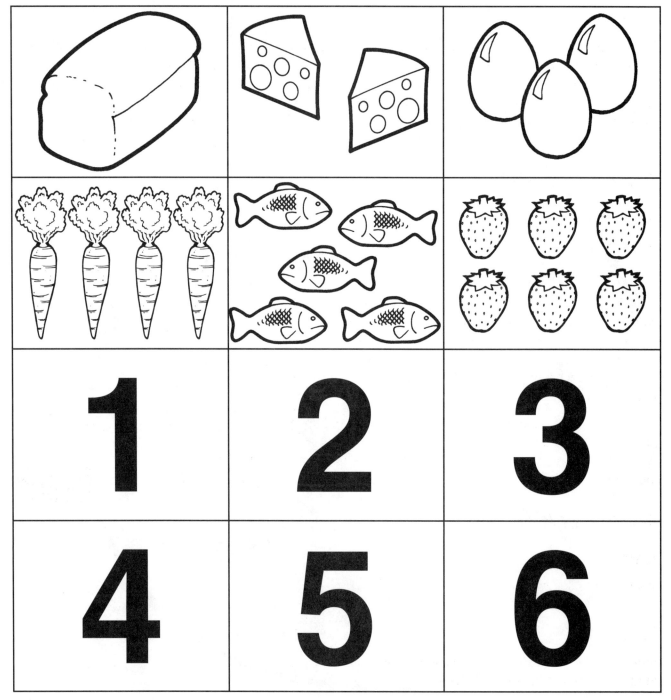

Count on Food

A number of foods lend themselves to hands-on math experiences. Here are three manipulative lessons for you to choose from and use with your class.

Computation

Materials

paper plates or shoebox lids; dried cereal, beans, or pasta; crayons or colored marking pens

Directions

Give each child a paper plate or box lid along with a handful of dried cereal, beans, or pasta. Let the children use their manipulatives to practice adding and subtracting basic facts or to count by twos, fives, etc. Or, direct the children to draw a scene on the inside of the box lids, for example, a picture of a garden with two flowers. Give each child a handful of bow-tie pasta. Tell a story problem and have the children follow along with their counters. For example, "Five butterflies (bow-tie pasta) sat on a flower. Two flew off. How many were left?"

Numeral Cut-outs

Materials

tagboard or cardboard; scissors; a variety of dried beans or rice; glue

Directions

Prepare tagboard or cardboard cutouts of any numeral. Direct the children to glue dried beans/rice to the numeral so that the numeral is completely covered with glued beans/rice. After the glue has dried instruct the children to trace the numerals with their fingers.

An alternative is to cut out the numerals and have the children glue a corresponding set of dried beans on each numeral (example: the numeral 2 = 2 dried beans). The numerals could then be used for counting or simple addition activities.

Tactile Numbers

Materials

shoebox lids; dry rice or orzo pasta

Directions

Pour enough rice in each lid to just cover the bottom of the lid. Direct the children to practice drawing numerals from one to ten in the rice.

Foods Around the World

Some of the foods we eat come from foreign countries. Read about each food. Draw and color a picture. Find the countries on a map of the world.

1. **Piroshkis** is a type of sandwich eaten in the **Ukraine**. Draw some potatoes and meat in the crust.

6. The **Chinese** eat plenty of **rice**. Draw some rice in the bowl.

2. **Spaghetti** is a favorite dish in **Italy**. Draw some spaghetti on the plate.

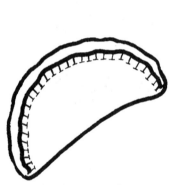

5. **Empanadas** are a favorite sandwich in **Chile**. Draw some meat in the crust.

3. In **Japan**, **fish** is often eaten raw. Draw some fish on the plate.

4. Boys and girls in **Great Britain** enjoy **jam sandwiches**. Draw some jam on the bread.

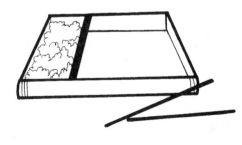

56

Pastabilities

Pasta comes in a wide variety of shapes. For example, there are shells, wheels, bow-ties, thick and thin rods, stars, and letters of the alphabet. These different shapes can be used to create the two art projects described below.

Golden Treasure Boxes

Materials

small cardboard boxes with lids (cigar boxes, shoe boxes, etc.); marking pen; assortment of pasta; white glue; gold spray paint; butcher paper

Directions

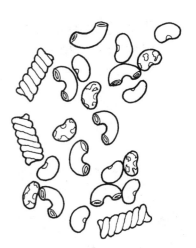

1. Spread butcher paper on the working surface. Give each child a cardboard box (write the child's name on the bottom of the box), glue, and some pasta.

2. Direct the children to squeeze some glue onto one side of the outside of the box and press pasta shapes onto the glue; allow the side to dry thoroughly. Continue in this manner until all four sides and the top of the box are covered with glued-on pasta. (The more densely the box is covered, the better the outcome.)

3. Take the pasta-covered boxes outside and spray paint them with gold spray paint; dry until paint is set. Bring the boxes indoors to dry completely.

Wearable Pasta

Materials

newspaper; smocks or old shirts; variety of dry pasta shapes; tempera paints, in a variety of colors; brushes; waxed paper; craft yarn; scissors

Directions

1. Cover the working surface with newspaper. Have the children put on their smocks. Direct them to paint the outside of the pasta and place the painted pasta tubes on the waxed paper to dry.

2. Cut the yarn into 18" (46 cm) lengths. Have the children thread their dried pastas onto the craft yarn. When they have as many tubes on their necklaces as they would like, tie the loose ends of the yarn together and wear as a necklace.

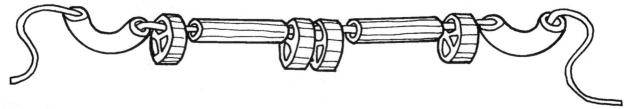

Note: You can have the children create a color pattern necklace by having them choose from a variety of colored pasta tubes. (Example: green, green, yellow, green, green, yellow)

Food Play

Sometimes children have to be admonished to stop playing with their food. Turn the tables and encourage the children to "play" with their food.

Edible Jewelry

Materials

string licorice; "O" cereal (any shape that has have a hole through the middle of the shape); butcher paper

Directions

1. Cover the working surface with butcher paper. Give each child a length of licorice (long enough for a necklace or a bracelet) and a handful of cereal.

2. Help the children make a large knot at one end of the licorice. Then have them thread the cereal onto the licorice string.

3. When the children have finished putting the cereal onto the licorice, tie the two ends of the licorice together in a knot. The children can then sample cereal from their jewelry during the day. (Note: Remind them not to bite through the licorice or the necklaces or bracelets will fall off!)

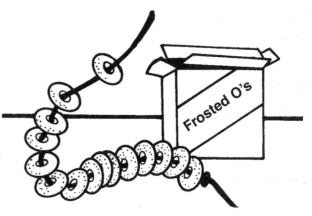

Pudding Paintings

Materials

prepared chocolate or butterscotch pudding (cook your own or look for pre-made containers in the dairy section of the grocery store); waxed paper; butcher paper; spoons; a smock for each child

Directions

1. Cover the working surface with butcher paper. Tell the children to put on their smocks and have them wash their hands.

2. Place a sheet of waxed paper in front of each child. Spoon a glob of chocolate pudding on each sheet of paper.

3. Direct the children to make a fingerpaint picture or design in their pudding. Tell them it is okay to lick their fingers clean before they wash up.

Table Manners

Throughout this food and nutrition unit you will be eating and sampling foods. Use this opportunity to introduce a closely-related skill—table manners. Here are some fun and easy activities to include in your lessons.

Goops

Read aloud the poem "Table Manners–I" from the book *Goops & How to Be Them* by Gelett Burgess (Dover Publications, Inc., 1968). Discuss whether or not the Goops display proper table manners. Talk about table manners and the use of "please" and "thank you." Plan a meal where good table manners are encouraged and used. Role-play meal times and practice using good manners and the words "please" and "thank you."

Placemats

Make placemats as directed below that will teach children where to place plates, cups, and utensils at meal times.

Materials

12" x 18" (30 cm x 46 cm) sheets of construction paper; black marking pen; plate, cup or glass; knife; fork; spoon; napkin; laminating material

Directions

1. Arrange the plate, cup, utensils, and napkin in correct position on a sheet of construction paper. With the marking pen, trace a dark line around each item. Remove all of the utensils.

2. Repeat the process to make subsequent placemats. When all of the mats have been completed, laminate them. Trim the edges.

3. Give each child one of the placemats at snack time (or create a planned eating time). Let them set their own places (fork, knife, spoon, napkin, cup, plate) using the mats as a guide.

Have children role-play waiters/waitresses and serve food items. During the role playing time, the children being served should by saying "please" and "thank you" when it is appropriate. Make certain all the children get a chance to be a waiter/waitress, as well as being served.

Food Safety

Discuss these food safety rules with the children. Display and practice these rules in your classroom every time you work with food.

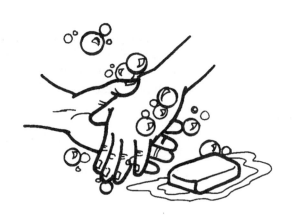

Wash your hands in hot, soapy water before you touch food.

Cover your mouth and nose when you sneeze. Be careful to turn your head away from food. Then wash your hands.

Scrub foods with a food brush before cutting or preparing them.

Wash cutting boards with a disinfectant after each use.

Pizza Party

Pizza can be part of a nutritious meal if it's not loaded down with too much cheese or other fatty foods. Teach the children how to cook a healthy, yet easy, pizza. Follow up with the quiz below.

Recipe

Ingredients

English muffins; lean ham or other luncheon meat; thinly sliced vegetable pieces (mushrooms, broccoli, etc.); diced tomatoes; Mozarella and grated Parmesan cheese

Directions

1. Let the children top their own muffins. Give each child one half of an English muffin. Instruct the children to place the ham on the muffin first. Add some vegetable pieces and diced tomatoes. Sprinkle with Mozarella and Parmesan cheese.
2. Broil the prepared muffins in a toaster oven until cheese is golden brown.

Quiz

On chart paper or the chalkboard copy the diagram below. Read the chart with the class. Ask the children to explain how they made their pizzas using their ingredients. Which food groups did they use? Which food group did they use first? second? third? fourth? last?

Let's Get Physical

Along with a healthy diet, we need exercise to stay fit. Here are some fun ways to include exercise in your curriculum.

Hot Potato

Scrub the outside of as many large potatoes as you will need. Divide the children into small groups. Instruct the groups to get in a circle. Tell the class that you have some hot potatoes. When a player is tossed the hot potato, he/she must quickly pass it to the person to his/her left so that they do not get "burned." Continue passing the hot potato from one player to another until you signal the potatoes must stop. Whomever is holding a potato is out and must go to the center of the circle. (**Note:** For fairness, do not face the children when you blow the whistle.)

Jump Rope Rhymes

Let the children jump rope to this food rhyme:

> **Fruits and veggies are good for me.**
> **They help me grow and keep me lean.**
> **Bread and rice are good to eat.**
> **As snacks or meals,**
> **They can't be beat.**

Hop Scotch

With chalk, draw a food pyramid on an outdoor blacktop area or make an indoor food pyramid with masking tape. Write the name of the appropriate food group in each section. For a game piece, use a small bean bag. After a player throws the game piece onto the board, he/she must name a food that belongs to that group before he or she can hop to that section. As each child moves his or her bean bag, he or she must name a food from all the food groups that he or she has visited thus far, as well as the new one the bean bag has just landed on.

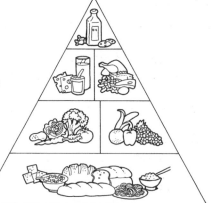

Pantomimes

Eating right is very important, but so is proper exercise. Have the children pantomime some physical activities. Whisper an action word (see examples below) to a child. After the action it has been performed, the others in the class guess the physical action. Whomever guesses the action correctly gets the next turn at pantomiming.

⎯ Action Words ⎯

running	pitching	jumping rope
bike riding	catching	dancing
swimming	surfing	batting
walking	skipping	skating

Food Fair

Invite other classes and families to your Food Fair. Participants can play a food game, make an art project, and create their own treat. Follow the directions below to help you organize this special event.

You may want to enlist the help of some adults to make the Food Fair run smoothly.

Planning

1. Write a class letter to send home to families, or to other classes inviting them to the big event. Be sure to tell them about some of the activities that they can expect to see and do.

2. Construct and display the Food Pyramid Bulletin Board (see pages 68-75).

3. Prepare the Healthy Eaters Game and Game Board. See pages 64 to 67 for directions and patterns. Place the completed project and playing directions on a table.

4. Plan which food samples you will have on hand—fruit kabobs (page 38) or vegetable treats (page 12). They can made by the children and would be a fun and easy for them to prepare.

5. Set up a number of display tables or centers to show off the food projects your children have made throughout this unit (poems, crafts, big books, etc.). When guests arrive they can visit the various centers and begin to participate in the different center activities.

6. After completing the food fair activities, send home the Nutrtion Newsletter (page 77).

Centers

You may want to set up the following centers or design some of your own:

1. **Game Center** where participants can play the Healthy Eaters Game (see page 64), rate their food habits, and test their knowledge of planning a healthy meal.

2. **Art Center** where everyone can make their own piece of Edible Jewelry (see page 58).

3. **Food Center** where guests can create their own treat. Serve yogurt and supply a number of toppings such as cereal, granola, raisins, and fruit.

4. **Writing Center** to display your class writing projects such as big books, poems, and innovations. Have children available at this center to read books or recite poetry to the guests.

Healthy Eaters Game

Guests at your Food Fair can rate their eating habits with a simple game. Let them choose food cards and match them up to a special chart. They will know at a glance if they are choosing healthy foods to eat.

Preparation

1. Make a copy of the food cards on pages 65 and 66 (do not cut cards apart yet). Color the pictures; glue card sheets to tagboard; allow to dry. Then laminate them and cut out. Store the prepared food cards in a specially-marked manila envelope.

2. Prepare a food chart game board as directed on page 67. The food chart may be colored. Glue it to tagboard; allow to dry. Laminate the chart for durability; trim the edges.

3. Make a copy of the directions (below). Place the directions, food cards and the food chart game board on the table (see diagram at right).

    Note: To extend the game card possibilities, let the children make additional food cards by gluing pictures to index cards and using as additional game cards.

How To Play

Teach your children how to play the healthy food game before the guests arrive. Display these directions at your Healthy Eaters Game Center. Have children at the center who can teach and help the guests play the game.

Directions for the Healthy Eaters Game

Choose some foods from the Food Cards that you think will make a healthy breakfast, lunch, or dinner. Match the food cards to the chart by placing your foods in the blank spaces. If most of the foods for your meal are in the bottom half of the chart, you have chosen a healthy meal. If most of the foods you chose for your meal are in the top half of the chart, you may want to try again (your meal is not very healthy).

Food Cards

Food Cards *(cont.)*

Game Board

Copy the food pyramid pattern below by enlarging to 200%. Cut out pyramid and glue to tagboard; laminate.

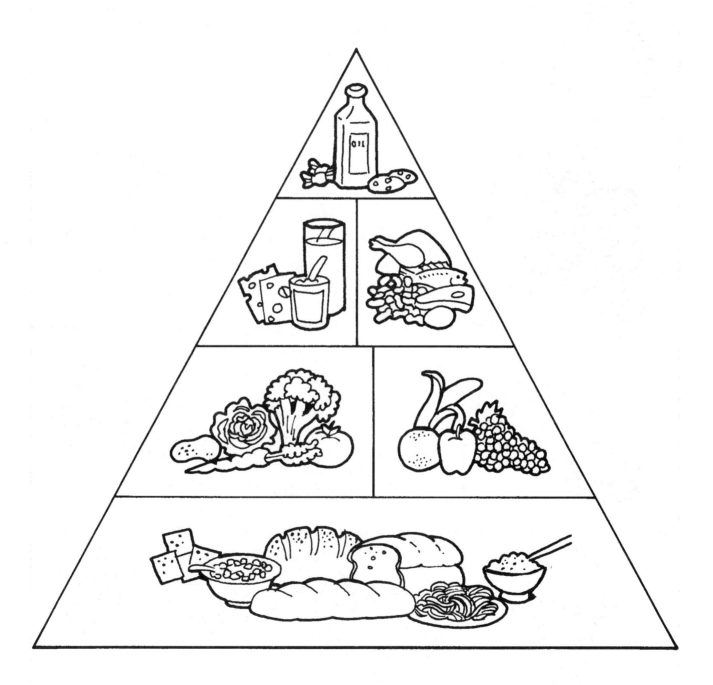

Food Pyramid Bulletin Board

Make a food pyramid bulletin board with the patterns on pages 69 to 75. Follow the easy step-by-step directions below.

Directions

1. Make copies of all pages from 69 to 75. (**Note:** Pages 74 and 75 are meant to be placed side-by-side when displayed.) Prepare a bulletin-board background with butcher paper, fabric, or any other chosen material.

2. Cut out each picture on the solid straight lines and color the foods shown. (For a pastel effect, rub a piece of art chalk along the inside border of each picture. Wipe the chalk with your finger or a tissue to create a translucent effect.) Assemble the pictures onto the prepared bulletin board background.

3. Add pictures or child-created drawings to each food group section as you progress through your food unit.

Extensions

1. Cover up the pictures on each bulletin board pattern before copying so that it will be reproduced as a "blank" food chart. Let the children cut out pictures from old magazines to glue onto the proper sections.

2. Prepare the bulletin board pieces and assemble them onto a large sheet of poster board. Color the foods. Laminate the whole sheet for more durability. Write on the laminate with wipe-off pens as you learn new facts and food group items.

3. Cut strips from construction paper. Make separate labels for all the foods pictured on the bulletin board. Attach a piece of Velcro® to the back of each label strip and attach the Velcro mate to the space below or next to each food picture. Let the children match the names to the foods by attaching the label strips to the correct food picture.

Food Pyramid Bulletin Board *(cont.)*

Fats, Oils, and Sweets

Use very little.

Food Pyramid Bulletin Board *(cont.)*

Milk, Yogurt, and Cheese
2–3 Servings

70

Food Pyramid Bulletin Board *(cont.)*

Meat, Poultry, Fish, Eggs, Dry Beans, and Nuts

2–3 Servings

Food Pyramid Bulletin Board *(cont.)*

Vegetables

3–5 Servings

Food Pyramid Bulletin Board *(cont.)*

Fruit

2–4 Servings

Food Pyramid Bulletin Board *(cont.)*

Bread, Cereal,
6–11 Servings

Food Pyramid Bulletin Board *(cont.)*

Rice, and Pasta

Cooking in the Classroom

Cooking in the classroom may take some time and preparation, but it can be made easier with the help of quick and easy recipes. Here are some cookbooks that were written especially for use with young children. They're sure to help you with your plans for classroom cooking activities.

Betty Crocker's Cooking with Kids. (Macmillan, 1995).

Cooking with Justin. by Justin Miller (Andrews & McMeel, 1997).

First Food Made Fun. by Miriam Stoppard (Dorling Kindersley, 1994).

Good Housekeeping's Illustrated Children's Cookbook. by Marianne Zanzarella (Morrow Junior Books, 1997).

Kids Cook! Fabulous Food for the Whole Family. by Sarah Williamson and Zachary Williamson (Williamson Publishing Company, 1992).

A Kid's Cookbook. Educational and Edible Delights. by Carol Kurzweg (Good Year Books, 1993). **Note.** This book contains a pullout poster of the food pyramid.

Kids Multicultural Cookbook. by Deanna F. Cook (Williamson Publishing Company, 1995).

Messpies. Microwave Cookbook of Deliciously Messy Masterpieces. by Lynn Gordon (Random House, 1996).

Mudliscious. Stories and Activities Featuring Food for Preschool Children. by Jan Irving and Robin Currie (Libraries Unlimited, Inc., 1986).

Pretend Soup and Other Real Recipes. by Mollie Katzen and Ann Henderson (Tricycle Press, 1994).

Extensions

Terms

Learn about some common cooking terms. Make an illustrated classroom chart of these words.

Class Book

Have each child bring in a favorite family snack recipe (cookie, vegetable, healthy, etc.). Glue each recipe onto a separate sheet of typing paper. Let the children draw pictures along the border of these pages. Punch holes along one side of the papers. Compile the recipes into a three-ring binder to make a classroom snack recipe book.